Adele

EXPECT
WONDERFUL
THINGS !

Happy 40th Birthday.
Love, Maribeth xo

Other books by Meredith Gaston

The Art of Gratitude
101 Inspirations for Your Journey
101 Moments of Joy and Inspiration
Tucked In: For Everyone Having a Doona Day

EXPECT WONDERFUL THINGS

Meredith Gaston

Andrews McMeel Publishing®

a division of Andrews McMeel Universal

FELLOW ADVENTURERS,

This little book comes to you with much love and warmest wishes—filled with words of inspiration and joy, and brimming with wise and gentle moments to enrich and brighten your days.

A hundred-and-one times over, as I sought to bring these words to life with drawings, I was given a new chance to focus on the way our thoughts shape our worlds, and to cultivate the power of joy in my daily life. I hope that these life-affirming pages will be as much a pleasure to explore as they have been for me to create.

I have found in the process of creating this book that my life has become immensely more joyful, harmonious, and fulfilling in every way. Stepping out of the fast lane and taking time to truly enjoy the magic and beauty that life has to offer, in a spirit of gratefulness and joy, is true inspiration for the soul.

An inspired life is a life lived to the fullest. I hope that these words encourage you to reach out and take hold of the life you dream of—remembering that we only live once and that life is made to be experienced in all its beauty, complexity, simplicity, and splendor.

There is nothing more wonderful than loving the life you live, and letting life love you right back.

I thank my family and friends for enriching my world with their support and tenderness. I thank you too, reader, for taking the time to invite these moments into your life, and wish you every joy in watching your life flourish and transform.

With love,
Meredith

SET YOUR COURSE
BY THE STARS,
NOT BY THE LIGHTS
OF EVERY PASSING
SHIP.

Omar Bradley

IMAGINATION IS MORE IMPORTANT THAN KNOWLEDGE.

Albert Einstein

AND THE DAY
CAME WHEN THE
RISK IT TOOK TO
REMAIN TIGHT INSIDE
THE BUD WAS MORE
PAINFUL THAN THE
RISK IT TOOK TO BLOSSOM.

Anaïs Nin

THE BUTTERFLY
COUNTS NOT
MONTHS BUT
MOMENTS,
AND HAS TIME
ENOUGH.

Rabindranath Tagore

EVERYONE IS THE AGE OF THEIR HEART.

Guatemalan proverb

HAPPINESS IS A JOURNEY, NOT A DESTINATION.

Paul H. Dunn

EAT HEALTHILY,
SLEEP WELL,
BREATHE DEEPLY,
MOVE HARMONIOUSLY.

Jean-Pierre Barral

WE ARE ALWAYS GETTING READY TO LIVE BUT NEVER LIVING.

Ralph Waldo Emerson

When you do things
from your **soul**, you
feel a river moving
in you, a **joy**.

Rumi

THE ONLY
JOURNEY
IS THE ONE
WITHIN.

Rainer Maria Rilke

THE GOAL IS
NOT TO SAIL
THE BOAT, BUT
RATHER TO HELP
THE BOAT SAIL
HERSELF.

John Rousmaniere

LET THE
BEAUTY OF
WHAT YOU LOVE
BE WHAT YOU
DO.

R u m i

There is only one
person who could ever
make you happy,
and that person is you.

David Burns

NEVER
GIVE UP!

As you walk,
eat, and travel,
be where you are.
Otherwise you
will miss most of
your life.

Buddha

THERE ARE NO MISTAKES

ONLY LESSONS.

Chinese proverb

REJOICE IN THE
WAY THINGS ARE.
WHEN YOU REALIZE
THERE IS NOTHING
LACKING, THE WHOLE
WORLD BELONGS TO YOU.

Lao Tzu

LEARN FROM YESTERDAY, LIVE FOR TODAY, HOPE FOR TOMORROW.

Albert Einstein

LIFE IS NOT ABOUT FINDING OURSELVES. LIFE IS ABOUT CREATING OURSELVES.

George Bernard Shaw

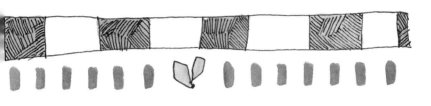

WHEREVER YOU GO, GO WITH ALL YOUR HEART.

Confucius

BE WHAT YOU ARE LOOKING FOR.

NOTHING IS
IMPOSSIBLE

TO A WILLING
HEART.

John Heywood

DERIVE STRENGTH FROM THOSE WHO LOVE AND SUPPORT YOU.

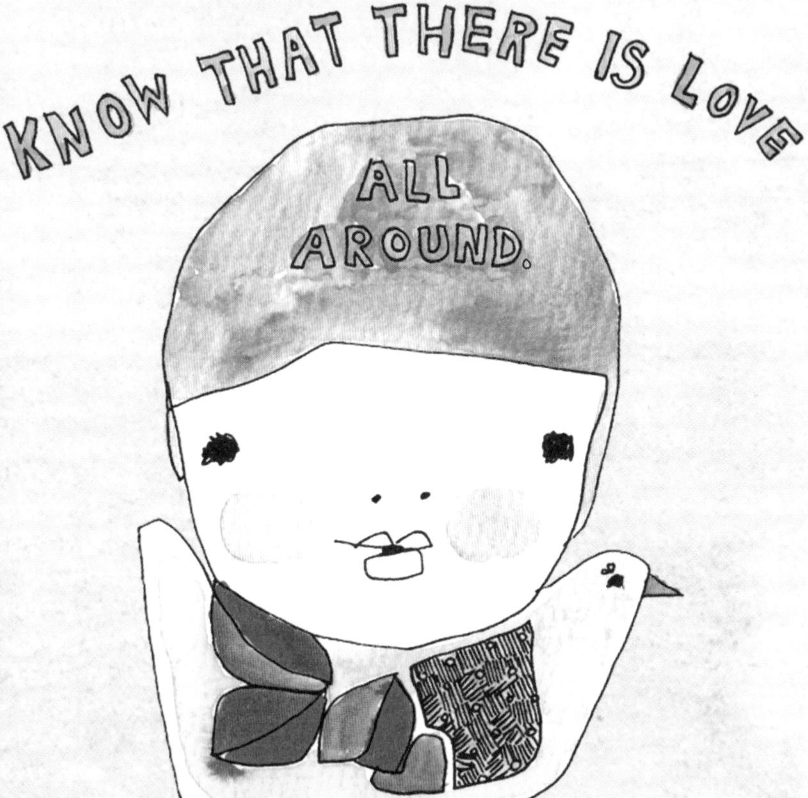
KNOW THAT THERE IS LOVE
ALL
AROUND.

KEEP YOUR FACE
ALWAYS TOWARD
THE SUNSHINE AND
SHADOWS WILL FALL
BEHIND YOU.

Walt Whitman

COME FORTH INTO THE LIGHT OF THINGS, LET NATURE BE YOUR TEACHER.

William Wordswort

SOMETIMES YOU HAVE TO BE YOUR OWN HERO.

LIVE EACH DAY
TO THE FULLEST,

ENJOY WHAT LIFE
HAS TO OFFER.

THOUGH WE
TRAVEL THE WORLD
OVER TO FIND THE
BEAUTIFUL,
WE MUST CARRY
IT WITH US, OR WE
FIND IT NOT.

Ralph Waldo Emerson

ADOPT THE PACE OF NATURE: HER SECRET IS PATIENCE.

Ralph Waldo Emerson

BE NOT FORGETFUL
TO ENTERTAIN
STRANGERS, FOR
THEREBY SOME
HAVE ENTERTAINED
ANGELS UNAWARES.

Hebrews 13:2

ALL OF OUR DREAMS
CAN COME TRUE,
IF WE HAVE THE COURAGE
TO PURSUE THEM.

Walt Disney

GRATITUDE
IS THE
OPEN DOOR
TO
ABUNDANCE.

TODAY YOU ARE
YOU, THAT IS TRUER
THAN TRUE, THERE
IS NO ONE ALIVE
WHO IS YOUER THAN
YOU.

Dr. Seuss

✦

BE YOURSELF.
EVERYONE ELSE IS
ALREADY TAKEN.

Oscar Wilde

GO CONFIDENTLY IN

LIVE THE LIFE

THE DIRECTION OF YOUR DREAMS.

YOU'VE IMAGINED.

Henry David Thoreau

EXPECT
WONDERFUL
THINGS
TO
HAPPEN.

Expect Wonderful Things

Copyright © 2017 by Meredith Gaston. All rights reserved.
Printed in China. No part of this book may be used
or reproduced in any matter whatsoever
without written permission except in the case
of reprints in the context of reviews.

Andrews McMeel Publishing
a division of Andrews McMeel Universal
1130 Walnut Street, Kansas City, Missouri 64106

www.andrewsmcmeel.com

17 18 19 20 21 SDB 10 9 8 7 6 5 4 3 2 1

ISBN : 978-1-4494-8052-3

Library of Congress Control Number : 2016944563

EXPECT WONDERFUL THINGS first appeared in
101 Moments of Joy and Inspiration, published by
Lantern, an imprint of Penguin Group, (Australia)

Editor : Patty Rice
Art Director and Designer: Julie Barnes
Production Editor : Mariah Marsden
Production Manager : Tamara Haus

ATTENTION SCHOOLS AND BUSINESSES

Andrews McMeel Books are available at quantity
discounts with bulk purchase for educational,
business, or sales promotional use.

For information, please e-mail the Andrews McMeel Publishing
Special Sales Department: specialsales@amuniversal.com.